Lunchboxes

To my children, Nicholas, Lara and Scarlett

Lunchboxes

*Quick, easy and
healthy ideas to
make lunchtime fun*

annabel karmel

The Random House Group Limited Reg. No. 954009

A CIP catalogue record for this book is available from the British Library

ISBN: 978-009-195581-6

Printed in Hong Kong

Eddison•Sadd Editions
CREATIVE DIRECTOR Nick Eddison   INDEXER Dorothy Frame
SENIOR EDITOR Katie Golsby   DESIGNER Brazzle Atkins
PROOFREADER Nikky Twyman   ILLUSTRATIONS Nadine Wikenden
PRODUCTION Sarah Rooney
COVER PHOTOGRAPHY Dave King

Notes on the text:
· For fan-assisted ovens, reduce the temperature by 20°C.
· All black pepper is freshly ground.

Contents

Introduction 6

Salads 12

Sandwiches 37

Savouries 65

Sweet treats 80

Index 94

About the author 95

Acknowledgements 95

Introduction

Children of school age consume one third of their daily food intake at school, so it's important that the bulk of the food in your child's lunchbox provides nutrients, vitamins and minerals for energy and growth. Unfortunately, of the 5½ billion children's lunchboxes packed each year, three quarters are overloaded with fat, sugar and salt. A healthy lunchbox should contain the following:

- a source of protein, such as chicken or tuna, to keep your child alert
- complex carbohydrates – for example, a pasta salad or a sandwich made with wholegrain bread – for energy
- a calcium-rich food, such as cheese or yoghurt, for healthy bones and teeth
- two portions of fruit and vegetables, for vitamins and minerals
- a little fat, for staying power – so, it's fine to include a treat, such as a cereal bar or some cookies, but it's best if these are home-made.

Children are all different but, by and large, what they want is a quick fix – a packet of crisps and a chocolate biscuit that can be wolfed down in minutes, saving as much time as possible for the playground.

It's highly unlikely that they will agree with their parents, that what they need is good food that will sustain them until lunchtime.

Healthy – and popular

Here are some suggestions on how to create a healthy lunchbox that *will* be eaten.

A sandwich with a difference

Sandwiches don't need to consist of ham or cheese slapped between two slices of soggy white bread. Supermarkets have helped enormously in recent years, by supplying bread from around the globe. Try giving pitta pockets with fillings like tuna, chopped egg, sweetcorn and mayonnaise. Try making sandwiches from ciabatta, bagels or mini baguettes. Tortilla wraps are the new trendy sandwich. My children love griddled chicken, shredded lettuce, tomato and salad cream, or prawns and shredded lettuce, with a cocktail sauce of mayonnaise mixed with a little ketchup, lemon juice and Worcestershire sauce.

Crunch and dip

Raw vegetables tend to be popular with children. Prepare sticks of carrot, sweet pepper, cucumber and so on, and wrap them in damp

kitchen paper to prevent them drying out.
With a tasty houmous dip, these are
surprisingly popular.

Salad in a box
Salads make a nice change from sandwiches. Try
Chicken Caesar Salad (*see page 18*), Chef's Salad with
Turkey and Cheese (*see page 13*), cherry tomatoes and
mini balls of mozzarella, or chicken salad with pasta,
sweetcorn, cherry tomatoes and spring onion.

Soup to go
As the colder weather sets in, it's a good idea
to include something hot in the lunchbox.
A wide-mouthed mini flask is ideal for
transporting a delicious cup of home-made
(or good-quality bought) soup like tomato or
minestrone (*see pages 74 and 77*), which are
both warming and nutritious. You could also
put foods like baked beans or pasta in a flask.

Fruity fun

Your child's lunch may be healthy, but it also needs to look appealing. Simple touches can make all the difference: whole fruit tends to be returned to sender, but bite-size chunks of fruit threaded onto a straw is likely to be a hit.

Playtime snacks

Crisps and chocolate biscuits tend to contain few nutrients and too much salt, sugar, additives and saturated fat. Instead, try offering Twiglets, popcorn, rice cakes, toasted seeds flavoured with honey and soy, yoghurt-covered raisins or dried apricots.

With some schools banning chocolate, cereal bars are often substituted for confectionery or biscuits. However, it is well worth checking the labels, as some cereal bars have a sugar content of more than 40 per cent, and a fat content of more than 30 per cent. Whereas the sugar eaten in a bowl of cereal tends to be washed away by the milk, with a sticky cereal bar the sugar sticks to the teeth, causing a lot more damage. For a more nutritious alternative, why not make your own flapjacks, cookies or muffins (*see pages 81–90*)?

What about a drink?

Pure fruit juice consists of 100 per cent fruit juice, as you would expect; however, a 'fruit juice drink' can contain as little as 5 per cent fruit juice. Many so-called 'juice drinks' are really only juice-flavoured sugary water, and contain more water and sugar than juice. Many also include artificial flavourings, sweeteners and colourings. Other good options are fresh-fruit smoothies, probiotic mini yoghurt drinks, or plain old water.

Recipe information

Where appropriate, the recipes in this book are accompanied by helpful information on preparation and cooking times, how many portions the recipe makes and whether it's suitable for freezing. Preparation times and portion quantities should be used as a guide only, as these will vary.

Preparation and packing

Lunches can be prepared the night before, to save time in the morning. You can prepare pasta salads or sandwich fillings, or include something from last night's dinner, like soup in a flask, chicken skewers or a frittata (Spanish omelette).

Salad dressings are best packed separately in a small plastic container, to be added to the salad at lunchtime. Otherwise, salads can become quite soggy and limp.

Lunchboxes left in a warm place can become a breeding ground for germs. To keep your child's lunchbox cool, put a mini ice pack or freezer gel pack in with his lunch. Alternatively, freeze a carton or plastic bottle of juice overnight, then put it in the lunchbox in the morning. This will help to keep food cool and will have defrosted by lunchtime. It's a good idea to buy an insulated lunchbox to keep the cold in and the heat out.

You will also need some plastic containers with lids that will fit inside your child's lunchbox. These are ideal for salads and prepared fruit and will prevent sandwiches from getting squashed. It's also a good idea to pop a small packet of wet wipes in the lunchbox.

Get your child involved

Try brainstorming some lunch ideas with your child, and plan what she is going to have in her lunchbox two or three days ahead. If you can, spend time together at the weekend preparing some food for the week ahead.

Salads

Chef's salad with turkey and cheese

To make the dressing, whisk together all the ingredients.

Mix together all the salad ingredients and toss in as much of the dressing as you like (there will probably be some left over).

/ 10 MINUTES

🍽 1 PORTION

❄ NOT SUITABLE FOR FREEZING

50 g (2 oz) cooked turkey, diced

4 cherry tomatoes, washed and halved

40 g (1½ oz) cucumber, washed and diced

½ little gem lettuce, washed and chopped

50 g (2 oz) Edam cheese, diced

1 spring onion, washed and finely sliced

½ punnet mustard and cress, washed

Dressing
1 teaspoon red wine vinegar

½ tablespoon runny honey

2 tablespoons olive oil

1 teaspoon orange juice

salt and pepper

As an alternative dressing, you could mix some mayonnaise with a little white wine vinegar.

Turkey pasta salad

/ 10 MINUTES

[::] 10 MINUTES

2–3 PORTIONS

NOT SUITABLE FOR FREEZING

50 g (2 oz) pasta shapes
50 g (2 oz) broccoli florets,
  washed
100 g (3½ oz) turkey or
  chicken breast fillet,
  cooked and chopped
100 g (3½ oz) tinned or
  frozen sweetcorn
2 tomatoes, skinned (see
  box, right), deseeded
  and chopped, or 6 cherry
  tomatoes, washed and
  halved
2 spring onions, thinly sliced

Dressing
3 tablespoons light olive oil
1 tablespoon runny honey
1 tablespoon soy sauce
1 tablespoon freshly
  squeezed lemon juice

Cook the pasta following the packet instructions.
Steam the broccoli florets for 5 minutes.

Meanwhile, whisk together all the ingredients
for the dressing.

Put the turkey or chicken, sweetcorn, tomatoes
and spring onions into a bowl, together with the
drained pasta, and toss with the dressing.

*To remove the skin from a tomato, cut a cross
in the base using a sharp knife. Put in a bowl
and cover with boiling water. Leave for 1 minute.
Drain and rinse in cold water. The skin should
peel off easily.*

Bow-tie pasta salad with chicken

Cook the pasta following the packet instructions. Add the broccoli and peas for the last 4 minutes of cooking time. Drain and refresh in cold water.

Mix the pasta and vegetables with the sweetcorn, chicken and cheese.

Mix together the dressing ingredients and pour over the pasta. Season to taste.

✎ 7 MINUTES

▦ 10 MINUTES

🍴 4 PORTIONS

❄ NOT SUITABLE FOR FREEZING

150 g (5 oz) bow-tie pasta
60 g (2 oz) broccoli florets, washed
50 g (2 oz) frozen peas
50 g (2 oz) tinned sweetcorn, drained
100 g (3½ oz) cooked chicken or ham, diced
50 g (2 oz) Emmenthal cheese, diced
salt and pepper

Dressing
3 tablespoons olive oil
1½ tablespoons white wine vinegar
1½ teaspoons caster sugar or honey
1 teaspoon soy sauce

Chicken Caesar salad

✎ 7 MINUTES

▭ 10 MINUTES

☕ 1 PORTION

❄ NOT SUITABLE FOR FREEZING

1 tablespoon olive oil
1 slice thick white bread
   (crusts removed), chopped
   into small cubes
1 chicken breast, chopped
   into bite-size pieces
1 little gem or ½ cos or
   romaine lettuce, washed
   and sliced
1 tablespoon Parmesan
   cheese, grated

Dressing
2 tablespoons mayonnaise
1 tablespoon grated
   Parmesan cheese
1 teaspoon lemon juice
½ small garlic clove, crushed
⅛ teaspoon Dijon mustard
a few drops of
   Worcestershire sauce
a few drops of Tabasco sauce

To make the croutons, heat the olive oil in a small non-stick frying pan and add the bread cubes. Fry, turning occasionally, until golden brown. Remove with a slotted spoon and drain on kitchen paper.

Put the chicken in the frying pan and fry for 4 minutes until cooked through. Leave to cool.

In a bowl, combine all the dressing ingredients and transfer to a water-tight container or bottle. Mix together the chicken and lettuce and put in a plastic container. Pack the grated Parmesan and the croutons in a separate container for your child to scatter over the salad at lunchtime. He will also need to mix in the dressing. This way, the salad will remain crisp.

The croutons and dressing can be made the evening before. Then all you need to do in the morning is sauté the chicken. You could even use ready-made croutons and cooked chicken breast.

Griddled chicken salad

🍴 3 MINUTES

🖥 15–20 MINUTES

🕒 4 PORTIONS

❄ SUITABLE FOR FREEZING

1 chicken breast fillet, skinned
1 tablespoon olive oil
1 teaspoon lemon juice
1 little gem lettuce, sliced
100 g (3½ oz) cherry tomatoes,
  washed and halved
1 avocado, peeled, stoned
  and diced
4 spring onions, washed
  and sliced

Dressing
2 tablespoons mayonnaise
2 tablespoons natural
  yoghurt
2 tablespoons olive oil
1 tablespoon tomato ketchup
½ teaspoon Dijon mustard
1 teaspoon white wine
  vinegar
4 tablespoons water
a pinch of sugar

Place the chicken on a chopping board and cover with a layer of clingfilm. Bash with a rolling pin to flatten it, then cut into 3 strips. Put the chicken into a bowl with the olive oil and lemon juice, then heat a griddle pan until hot. Cook the chicken for 2 minutes on each side, then slice into thin strips.

Put the lettuce, tomatoes, avocado and spring onions together in a bowl and mix, then add the chicken.

Mix together all the ingredients for the dressing and store in a container. Your child will need to drizzle the dressing over the salad at lunchtime.

You can also make this using ready-cooked chicken.

Chicken orzo pasta salad

Cook the pasta following the packet instructions, drain and refresh in cold water. Cook the green beans in boiling water for 4 minutes. Drain and refresh in cold water, then finely slice.

Mix together the pasta, green beans, tomatoes, sweetcorn, chicken, basil and Parmesan.

Combine the dressing ingredients and pour over the pasta. Toss together and season.

✏ 8 MINUTES

🖥 10 MINUTES

🍳 4 PORTIONS

❄ NOT SUITABLE FOR FREEZING

75 g (3 oz) orzo (rice-shaped pasta)
75 g (3 oz) green beans, washed
50 g (2 oz) cherry tomatoes, washed and halved
3 tablespoons tinned sweetcorn, drained
1 cooked chicken breast, diced
2 tablespoons chopped basil
20 g (¾ oz) Parmesan cheese, grated
salt and pepper

Dressing
1 tablespoon balsamic vinegar
1 tablespoon soy sauce
3 tablespoons olive oil
½ garlic clove, crushed

Chicken, broccoli and mangetout pasta salad

Cook the pasta following the packet instructions, adding the broccoli and mangetout 2 minutes before the end of the cooking time. Drain and then immediately rinse well with cold water. Drain again thoroughly.

In a large bowl, whisk together the oils, rice wine vinegar, honey and soy sauce. Add the pasta and vegetables and toss to coat. Cover and refrigerate until needed. Just before serving, add the chicken and toss again, then sprinkle with the pumpkin seeds.

3 MINUTES

10 MINUTES

2 PORTIONS

NOT SUITABLE FOR FREEZING?

110 g (4 oz) pasta spirals
65 g (2½ oz) small broccoli florets, washed
40 g (1½ oz) mangetout or sugarsnap peas, washed and sliced
3 tablespoons sunflower oil
½ teaspoon toasted sesame oil
2 teaspoons rice wine vinegar
2 teaspoons clear honey
2 teaspoons soy sauce
110 g (4 oz) cooked chicken, thinly sliced
3 tablespoons pumpkin seeds

Broccoli is rich in a wide range of nutrients, and helps to strengthen the immune system. Pumpkin seeds are a good source of essential fatty acids.

Chicken and rice salad

/ 7 MINUTES

[] 20 MINUTES

4 PORTIONS

NOT SUITABLE FOR FREEZING

150 g (5 oz) mixed white and
  wild rice
1 cooked chicken breast,
  diced
1 tomato, washed, deseeded
  and diced
4 spring onions, washed
  and thinly sliced
3 tablespoons tinned
  sweetcorn, drained
salt and pepper

Dressing
3 tablespoons olive oil
2 teaspoons white wine
  vinegar
1 teaspoon Dijon mustard
1 teaspoon caster sugar

Cook the rice following the packet instructions.
Drain and refresh in cold water, then tip into a
bowl. Add the remaining ingredients and season
to taste.

  Mix together the dressing ingredients and
drizzle over the rice.

*Rice contains starch that is digested and absorbed
slowly, which provides a steady blood sugar level
for long-lasting energy.*

Thai noodle salad

Cook the noodles according to the packet instructions. Mix together with the shredded chicken, cucumber and carrot strips, spring onion and sweetcorn.

Mix together the ingredients for the dressing and pour over the noodle salad.

/ 5 MINUTES

⬛ 20 MINUTES

☕ 4 PORTIONS

❄ NOT SUITABLE FOR FREEZING

125 g (4½ oz) egg noodles
1 small chicken breast, cooked and shredded
100 g (3½ oz) cucumber, seeds removed and cut into strips
75 g (3 oz) carrot, peeled and cut into strips
2 spring onions, finely sliced
100 g (3½ oz) tinned or cooked frozen sweetcorn

Dressing
3 tablespoons plum sauce
1 tablespoon rice wine vinegar
1 teaspoon honey
2 teaspoons sweet chilli sauce

Sweetcorn is high in fibre and vitamin C. Frozen sweetcorn may contain more nutrients than fresh corn from the supermarket.

Ham and chicken pasta salad

/ 10 MINUTES

⬚ 10 MINUTES

🥧 4 PORTIONS

❄ NOT SUITABLE FOR FREEZING

100 g (3½ oz) shell pasta
15 g (½ oz) carrot, peeled
  and grated
4 spring onions, washed
  and sliced
1 tomato, deseeded and
  diced
2 tablespoons tinned
  sweetcorn, drained
1 tablespoon fresh chopped
  basil
25 g (1 oz) ham, sliced
25 g (1 oz) cooked chicken,
  diced
salt and pepper

Dressing

1 tablespoon cider vinegar
3 tablespoons olive oil
2 teaspoons soy sauce
2 teaspoons honey

Cook the pasta following the packet instructions.
Drain and refresh in cold water. Mix with the
remaining salad ingredients.

  Mix together the ingredients for the dressing
and pour over the salad. Season to taste.

Bulgur wheat salad

🔪 5 MINUTES

⊞ 15 MINUTES

🍳 4 PORTIONS

❀ NOT SUITABLE FOR FREEZING

100 g (3½ oz) bulgur wheat
200 ml (7 fl oz) water
20 g (¾ oz) dried cranberries
4 spring onions, washed
    and sliced
1 tomato, deseeded and
    diced
2 tablespoons tinned
    sweetcorn, drained
100 g (3½ oz) cucumber,
    washed and diced
1 tablespoon chopped chives
1 tablespoon rice wine
    vinegar
2 tablespoons olive oil
a pinch of sugar

Put the bulgur wheat and water into a saucepan
and bring to the boil. Cover and remove from the
heat for 10 minutes until the water has absorbed.
Alternatively, follow the packet instructions. Add
the remaining ingredients and toss together.

*Bulgur wheat is a whole-wheat grain that has
been cracked and partially precooked. It's rich
in protein and minerals and has a nutty taste.
Different types of bulgur wheat require different
cooking times, so check the packet instructions.*

Carrot and cucumber salad

If using the sesame seeds, toast them in a dry frying pan, stirring occasionally, for a few minutes until golden.

Using a swivel vegetable peeler, slice the carrot and cucumber into thin strips.

Mix together the dressing ingredients and toss with the salad.

🔪 5 MINUTES
🍳 5 MINUTES
🍽 2 PORTIONS
❄ NOT SUITABLE FOR FREEZING

1 large carrot (about 150 g/
   5 oz), peeled
60 g (2 oz) cucumber

Dressing
1 tablespoon sesame seeds
   (optional)
1 tablespoon soy sauce
1 tablespoon rice wine
   vinegar
1 tablespoon sunflower oil
1 tablespoon runny honey
1 teaspoon mirin
1 teaspoon sesame oil

The Japanese make this salad using seaweed and cucumber. However, seaweed is pretty hard to find, so I've used carrot instead. You could also use beansprouts or shredded Chinese cabbage.

Confetti couscous salad

Toast the pine nuts in a dry frying pan, stirring occasionally, for a few minutes until golden.

Put the couscous into a bowl. Pour over the stock and leave to stand for about 5 minutes or according to the packet instructions.

Fluff up the couscous with a fork. Stir in the pepper, carrot, spring onion, raisins and pine nuts.

Whisk together the dressing ingredients and stir into the couscous. Season to taste.

✏ 5 MINUTES
▢ 10 MINUTES
◔ 2 PORTIONS
❄ NOT SUITABLE FOR FREEZING

1½ tablespoons pine nuts
45 g (1½ oz) couscous
125 ml (4 fl oz) hot vegetable stock
20 g (¾ oz) red pepper, washed, deseeded and diced
½ medium carrot (50 g/2 oz), peeled and diced
2 spring onions, washed and sliced
1 tablespoon raisins

Dressing
1 tablespoon olive oil
1½ teaspoons lemon juice
½ teaspoon honey
salt and pepper

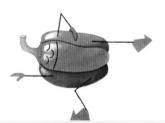

Couscous is a form of grain made from wheat and is popular in Middle Eastern cuisine. It's fairly high in minerals and vitamins and is very quick and easy to prepare.

Yummy salmon and rice salad

⟋ 10 MINUTES, PLUS 30
MINUTES FOR CHILLING

▢ 10 MINUTES

🍪 4 PORTIONS

❄ NOT SUITABLE FOR FREEZING

285 g (10 oz) salmon fillets,
  cut into chunks
400 ml (14 fl oz) fish stock
a knob of butter
200 g (7 oz) long grain rice
200 g (7 oz) frozen peas
1 red pepper, washed,
  deseeded and diced
½ cucumber, peeled and
  diced
1 small bunch spring onions,
  washed and sliced
2 tablespoons chopped
  flat-leaf parsley
2 tablespoons chopped dill
2 tablespoons chopped chives
2 tablespoons olive oil
2 tablespoons rice wine
  vinegar
2 teaspoons runny honey
salt and pepper

Put the salmon into a saucepan with the fish
stock and butter, and poach over a gentle heat
for about 7 minutes, or until the fish flakes easily
with a fork. Alternatively, place the salmon in a
microwave-proof dish and sprinkle with lemon
juice. Cover the dish with clingfilm and pierce
several times. Cook the salmon on High for about
2 minutes, or until it flakes easily. Allow to cool.

Cook the rice following the packet instructions,
adding the peas for the last 4 minutes of the
cooking time. Drain and refresh in cold water.

Put the remaining ingredients into a large
bowl. Add the rice and peas, then flake in the
cold salmon. Season well, then cover and chill
for 30 minutes before serving.

Salmon and dill pasta salad

/ 7 MINUTES

☐ 10 MINUTES

🍽 4 PORTIONS

❄ NOT SUITABLE FOR FREEZING

100 g (3½ oz) bow-tie pasta
50 g (2 oz) broccoli florets,
  washed
4 spring onions, washed
  and sliced
100 g (3½ oz) cucumber,
  peeled and diced
1 tablespoon chopped dill
150 g (5 oz) salmon fillet
juice of ½ a lemon
salt and pepper

Dressing
½ teaspoon Dijon mustard
1 tablespoon rice wine
  vinegar
2 tablespoons olive oil
1 teaspoon honey
½ teaspoon lemon juice

Cook the pasta following the packet instructions.
Add the broccoli 3 minutes before the end of the
cooking time. Drain, refresh in cold water, then
tip into a bowl. Add the spring onions, cucumber
and dill.

Put the salmon into a microwave-proof dish.
Add the lemon juice and cover with clingfilm.
Pierce several times, then cook in the microwave
on High for 2½ minutes until cooked. Leave to
cool, then flake into the pasta.

Mix together the dressing ingredients. Pour
over the pasta and season.

Tuna Niçoise salad

Bring a saucepan of water to the boil and cook the green beans for 4 minutes. Drain and refresh under cold water, then slice the beans into three.

In a large bowl, mix together the lettuce, green beans, tomatoes, egg, cucumber and tuna.

Combine the dressing ingredients in a jug, then season and pour over the salad.

✐ 10 MINUTES

🖩 5 MINUTES

🍴 4 PORTIONS

❄ NOT SUITABLE FOR FREEZING

75 g (3 oz) fine green beans, washed and topped and tailed
2 little gem lettuce, washed and sliced
100 g (3½ oz) cherry tomatoes, washed and halved
1 hard-boiled egg, shelled and quartered
¼ cucumber, peeled and diced
185 g (6½ oz) tinned tuna in sunflower oil, drained
salt and pepper

Dressing
1 teaspoon Dijon mustard
3 tablespoons olive oil
1 tablespoon white wine vinegar
1 teaspoon honey

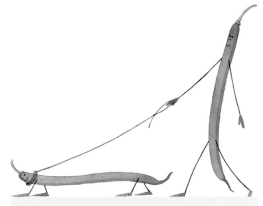

Tuna is a true superfood, rich in protein, vitamin D and vitamin B12, as well as omega-3 fatty acids, which help to protect against heart disease.

Orzo tuna salad

✎ 5 MINUTES

⊟ 10 MINUTES

☕ 4 PORTIONS

✳ NOT SUITABLE FOR FREEZING

75 g (3 oz) orzo pasta
50 g (2 oz) tinned tuna,
    drained
3 tablespoons tinned
    sweetcorn, drained
2 spring onions, washed
    and sliced
3 tablespoons chopped
    chives
½ teaspoon Dijon mustard
2 teaspoons rice wine
    vinegar
1 tablespoon olive oil
60 g (2 oz) light mayonnaise
salt and pepper

Cook the orzo following the packet instructions,
then drain and refresh in cold water. Tip into
a bowl, then add the tuna, sweetcorn, spring
onions and chives. Mix together the mustard,
rice wine vinegar, olive oil and mayonnaise. Add
to the salad with the seasoning, then combine.

Sandwiches

Sandwiches

There are now many types of bread available in the supermarket that can be used to make sandwiches. Try granary or wholemeal bread, pitta pockets, bagels, ciabatta or mini baguettes.

If you're usually in a rush in the morning, it will help if you get the ingredients together and make up your tuna mayonnaise, for instance, the night before.

To keep the sandwiches fresh, always wrap them in clingfilm or aluminium foil as soon as you've made them. To prevent the sandwiches getting squashed, store them in a small plastic container in your child's lunchbox.

Favourite sandwich fillings

- *50 g (2 oz) chicken breast mixed with 1 tablespoon mayonnaise, 1 sliced spring onion and 1 teaspoon lemon juice, and a little Cheddar cheese grated on top*
- *1 chopped hard-boiled egg mixed with 1 tablespoon mayonnaise and 1 rasher chopped bacon, and 4 slices of tomato on top*
- *Peanut butter, mashed banana and a little honey*
- *Marmite and grated Gruyère cheese*
- *Cream cheese, fruit chutney and cucumber*
- *Houmous and grated carrot*

- *Houmous, grated carrot and mature Cheddar cheese*
- *Plum sauce, sliced chicken, lettuce and cucumber*
- *Tuna and sweetcorn, spring onion, cucumber and mayonnaise*
- *Cream cheese, cucumber and smoked salmon*
- *Wafer-thin sliced ham or turkey and thinly sliced Swiss cheese*
- *Shredded roast chicken mixed with sweetcorn and chopped lean bacon and a little mayonnaise*

Egg mayo

 3 MINUTES

1 PORTION

1 large egg, hard-boiled
1 tablespoon mayonnaise
salt and pepper
1 teaspoon snipped chives
2 slices white bread,
    buttered

Mash the egg with the mayonnaise and seasoning. Add the chives and mix together. Spread over one slice of the bread, then sandwich with the other slice. Remove the crusts and cut into 6 fingers.

Prawn cocktail

 3 MINUTES

1 PORTION

2 tablespoons mayonnaise
2 teaspoons tomato ketchup
a dash of lemon juice
50 g (2 oz) small cooked
    prawns
salt and pepper
2 slices granary bread,
    buttered

Mix together the mayonnaise, tomato ketchup and lemon juice, then add the prawns and seasoning. Spread over one slice of the bread, then sandwich with the other slice. Remove the crusts and cut into 6 fingers.

Pastrami on rye

Mix together the mayonnaise, honey and mustard and season with black pepper. Spread over the rye bread. Lay the pastrami over one slice of bread. Scatter over the rocket and cover with the remaining bread. Cut in half.

3 MINUTES

1 PORTION

1 tablespoon mayonnaise
1/4 teaspoon honey
a pea-sized dot of Dijon
    mustard
freshly ground black pepper
2 slices rye bread
4 thin slices pastrami
a small handful of shredded
    rocket

BLT

Lightly toast the bread, then spread with the butter and the mayonnaise. Top one slice with the lettuce, tomato and bacon, then finish with the other slice. Cut into 4 triangles.

10 MINUTES

1 PORTION

2 slices white bread
a little butter, softened
1 tablespoon light
    mayonnaise
a little iceberg lettuce,
    washed and shredded
1 tomato, washed and sliced
20 g (3/4 oz) smoked streaky
    bacon, cooked

Toasted club sandwich

Toast the bread until lightly golden. Spread one side with the butter and mayonnaise. Arrange the turkey on one slice, then the lettuce. Put the second slice of toast on top (mayonnaise side up), followed by the egg, tomato and cheese. Put the third slice of bread on top and press together. Cut into 4 triangles.

✎ 15 MINUTES
🎨 1 PORTION

3 thin slices granary bread
a little butter, softened
a little light mayonnaise
2 slices cooked turkey
a little lettuce, washed
1 hard-boiled egg, sliced
1 tomato, washed and sliced
1 slice Emmenthal cheese

Mini bread rolls

Slice the rolls in half and butter lightly. Spread one side of each roll with pickle. Put the cheese on top, then the tomato and lettuce. Finish with the tops of the rolls.

✎ 3 MINUTES
🎨 4 MINI ROLLS

4 mini brown bread rolls
a little butter, softened
4 teaspoons pickle
50 g (2 oz) Cheddar cheese,
   grated
1 tomato, washed and sliced
a little iceberg lettuce,
   washed and shredded

Left: Toasted club sandwich

Cheese and tomato pinwheels

/ 3 MINUTES

 8 PINWHEELS

2 slices white or brown
 bread, crusts removed
a little butter, softened
50 g (2 oz) Cheddar cheese,
 grated
1 tomato, washed, deseeded
 and diced

Put the slices of bread on a chopping board and
cover with clingfilm. Using a wooden rolling pin,
roll out the bread until it is very thin. Spread with
butter and sprinkle over the cheese and tomato.
Roll up each slice (like a roulade) and cut into
4 pieces.

Cream cheese, mango and tomato pinwheels

/ 3 MINUTES

8 PINWHEELS

2 slices brown bread, crusts
 removed
2 dessertspoons cream
 cheese
1 teaspoon mango chutney
1 small tomato, washed,
 deseeded and diced

Roll out the bread as described above. Spread
with the cream cheese, then the mango chutney,
and sprinkle over the tomato. Roll up each slice,
as above, and cut into 4 pieces.

Lara's chicken wraps

Score the chicken with a sharp knife. Mix together all the ingredients for the marinade and marinate the chicken for about 20 minutes.

Brush a griddle pan with oil. Remove the chicken from the marinade and, when the griddle is hot, cook the chicken for about 4 minutes on each side or until cooked through. Cut the chicken into strips and set aside.

Spread each tortilla with 1 tablespoon of mayonnaise and arrange the chicken strips in a line down one side of the tortilla, about 4 cm (1½ in) from the edge of the tortilla. Place the shredded lettuce and strips of tomato in lines beside the chicken. Roll up and cut each tortilla in half and wrap in foil.

If serving at home, it's a good idea to warm the tortillas in the microwave for a few seconds before filling, to make them more pliable.

You could use ready-cooked chicken to save time.

 5 MINUTES, PLUS 20
MINUTES FOR MARINATING

 10 MINUTES

 4 WRAPS

2 chicken breast fillets
sunflower oil, for cooking
4 large flour tortillas (25 cm/ 10 in)
4 tablespoons mayonnaise
a handful of shredded iceberg lettuce, washed
4 tomatoes, washed and cut into strips
salt and pepper

Marinade
1 tablespoon olive oil
1 tablespoon fresh lemon juice
1 garlic clove, lightly crushed
1 tablespoon dark soy sauce
1 tablespoon clear honey
½ tablespoon brown sugar
2 tablespoons sunflower oil

Oriental plum chicken wraps

 7 MINUTES

 12 WRAPS

4 tablespoons mayonnaise
1 tablespoon plum sauce
4 large flour tortillas
1 cooked chicken breast, sliced
4 spring onions, washed and sliced into strips
¼ small cucumber, washed and sliced into thin strips

Mix the mayonnaise and plum sauce together. Warm the tortillas in the microwave for 20 seconds, or in a dry frying pan for about 15 seconds on each side.

Spread a little of the mayonnaise mixture along one half of each wrap. Top with chicken, spring onion and cucumber. Roll up, then slice diagonally into three pieces.

Quick turkey wrap

 3 MINUTES

 2 WRAPS

2 small flour tortillas (15 cm/ 6 in)
1 tablespoon salad cream or mayonnaise
2 thin slices of turkey
a handful of shredded lettuce, washed
2 heaped tablespoons grated cheese

Lay out the tortillas and spread with the salad cream or mayonnaise. Lay a turkey slice on each tortilla, cover with lettuce and cheese and roll up. Wrap with clingfilm.

Advise your child to unwrap the tortilla slowly as she eats, to keep the filling contained.

Right: Oriental plum chicken wraps

Southwestern chicken wrap

Place the chicken breast between two layers of clingfilm and, using a rolling pin, beat to make an escalope 5 mm (¼ in) thick.

Mix together the fajita seasoning, olive oil and lemon or lime juice and rub over the chicken. Leave to stand for 10 minutes.

Preheat the grill to High and grill the chicken, 12 cm (5 in) from the heat source, for 5–6 minutes on each side, until cooked through. Allow to cool, then refrigerate until needed. (This can be done up to 2 days in advance.)

Slice the cold chicken into thin strips. Mix together the sour cream, mayonnaise, lime juice and seasoning, and spread over the tortillas. Scatter the lettuce and tomato on top and lay the chicken strips down the centre, then roll up.

 15 MINUTES

10–12 MINUTES

2 WRAPS

NOT SUITABLE FOR FREEZING

125 g (4½ oz) skinless chicken breast fillet
1 teaspoon fajita seasoning
2 teaspoons olive oil
½ teaspoon lemon or lime juice, plus another ½ teaspoon lime juice
2 tablespoons sour cream
2 teaspoons mayonnaise
salt and pepper
2 large flour tortillas
a handful of shredded romaine or iceberg lettuce, washed
1 medium tomato, washed, deseeded and cut into strips

5 MINUTES

 1 WRAP

1 tablespoon light
  mayonnaise
1 large flour tortilla
30 g (1 oz) cooked chicken,
  sliced
1 tablespoon grated carrot
1 tablespoon grated
  Cheddar cheese
¼ avocado, peeled, stoned
  and sliced
½ teaspoon lemon juice

Chicken, avocado and carrot wrap

Spread the mayonnaise along one side of the wrap. Top with the chicken, carrot, Cheddar and avocado. Drizzle over the lemon juice. Roll up, then slice into 3 pieces.

 5 MINUTES

 1 WRAP

1½ tablespoons mayonnaise
1 teaspoon water
a little lemon juice
a few drops of
  Worcestershire sauce
1½ teaspoons grated
  Parmesan cheese
1 large flour tortilla
40 g (1½ oz) cooked chicken,
  shredded
2 tablespoons grated carrot
15 g (½ oz) lettuce, washed
  and shredded

Chicken Caesar wrap

To make the dressing, mix together the mayonnaise, water, lemon juice, Worcestershire sauce and Parmesan cheese. Then heat the tortilla in the microwave for 20 seconds, or in a dry frying pan for about 15 seconds on each side.

  Mix together the chicken and grated carrot and toss with the dressing. Arrange along one side of the tortilla. Top with the lettuce and roll up.

Tomato, mozzarella and pesto wrap

Mix together the pesto and mayonnaise and spread over the tortilla. Pat the tomato dry on a paper towel, then layer the tomato and mozzarella down the centre. Season with salt and pepper and a drizzle of olive oil, if using. Roll up and cut in half.

 5 MINUTES

 2 WRAPS

1 teaspoon pesto
1 tablespoon mayonnaise
1 wheat tortilla (18 cm/7 in)
1 large tomato, skinned, deseeded and finely sliced
60 g (2 oz) mozzarella cheese, sliced
salt and pepper
a drizzle of olive oil (optional)

Pastrami, dill pickle and tomato wrap

Warm the tortillas in the microwave for 20 seconds and place on a board. Spread 1 tablespoon of mayonnaise over one half of each tortilla. On top of the mayonnaise, put 2 slices of pastrami, half the dill pickle or gherkin slices, half the tomato slices and half the lettuce. Add some seasoning, then roll up the tortillas. Diagonally slice each wrap into two.

🖊 5 MINUTES

 2 PORTIONS

2 large flour tortillas
2 tablespoons light
  mayonnaise
4 thin slices of pastrami
1 dill pickle or gherkin, thinly
  sliced
1 tomato, washed, deseeded
  and sliced
a handful of shredded
  green lettuce, washed
salt and pepper

It's a good idea to wrap one end of the tortilla in foil so that the filling doesn't fall out when it's eaten. Your child can unfold the foil as he eats the wrap.

Kiddy sushi-style rolls

 7 MINUTES

 1 PORTION

2 slices white bread, crusts removed
80 g (3 oz) tinned tuna in sunflower oil, drained
2 tablespoons mayonnaise
1½ tablespoons tomato ketchup
a few drops of Tabasco sauce
5 cm (2 in) length of cucumber, washed and cut into strips
5 cm (2 in) length of carrot, peeled and coarsely grated

Using a rolling pin, flatten the bread until it is about 5 mm (¼ in) thick.

Mix the tuna together with 1 tablespoon of the mayonnaise, the tomato ketchup and the Tabasco sauce. Spread the remaining mayonnaise over the bread and then spoon the tuna in a line about 1.5 cm (½ in) from one edge of the bread. Arrange the cucumber strips on one half of the tuna and the grated carrot on the other half. Roll up, starting from the filled side, and press down to seal. Trim the ends to neaten using a sharp knife, then cut into three little rolls.

Other good fillings to try are:
- *Tinned salmon, mayonnaise, tomato ketchup and chopped spring onion with cucumber strips*
- *Strips of Cheddar cheese with slices of tomato and cucumber*
- *Houmous with grated carrot, shredded lettuce and chopped tomato*

Prawn and avocado wrap

🔪 7 MINUTES

🍪 2 WRAPS

¼ avocado, peeled, stoned
  and chopped
1 teaspoon lemon juice
½ medium tomato, washed,
  deseeded and chopped
1 teaspoon sliced spring
  onion
30 g (1 oz) small cooked
  prawns
1 tablespoon mayonnaise
½ teaspoon tomato ketchup
salt and pepper
1 large flour tortilla

Put the avocado and lemon juice into a small
bowl and toss together until the avocado is well
coated. Add the tomato, spring onion, prawns,
mayonnaise and tomato ketchup, and combine.
Season with salt and pepper.

Spoon the mixture onto the tortilla and roll
it up, then cut it in half.

Chicken pitta pockets

Mix together the lemon juice, sour cream, chives, spring onion and chicken, and season to taste. Cut the pitta bread in half and open up the pockets. Spoon in the mixture and add the lettuce and tomato.

 7 MINUTES

2 PITTA POCKETS

½ teaspoon lemon juice
1½ tablespoons sour cream
1 teaspoon chopped chives
1 spring onion, washed and sliced
30 g (1 oz) cooked chicken, sliced
salt and pepper
1 pitta bread
a little lettuce, washed and shredded
4 cherry tomatoes, washed, deseeded and sliced

If your child is a fussy eater, it can be much better to give her a packed lunch containing the food she likes rather than letting her go hungry because she doesn't like school lunches.

Pitta pocket with tuna and sweetcorn

✎ 5 MINUTES

▥ 10 MINUTES

🍪 4 PITTA POCKETS

2 eggs
200 g (7 oz) tinned tuna
  in sunflower oil, drained
100 g (3½ oz) tinned
  sweetcorn, drained
2 tablespoons mayonnaise
1 teaspoon white wine
  vinegar
4 spring onions, washed
  and chopped
salt and pepper
a few drops of Tabasco
  sauce
a handful of salad cress
  (optional)
2 pitta breads

Put the eggs in a saucepan of cold water and bring to the boil. Reduce the heat and simmer for 7–8 minutes. Drain and cool under cold water. Peel the eggs when cold.

Meanwhile, flake the tuna with a fork and mix with the sweetcorn, mayonnaise, white wine vinegar, spring onions, salt and pepper and Tabasco sauce. Roughly chop the hard-boiled eggs and add to the tuna mix with the salad cress (if using), stirring well.

Cut the pitta breads in half to make 4 pitta pockets, then open them up and divide the mixture equally.

Smoked salmon and cream cheese bagel

🖌 3 MINUTES

🍽 1 PORTION

Mix together the cream cheese and chives and spread over both halves of the bagel. Lay the salmon and cucumber (if using) on top and finish with a little lemon juice and pepper (if using).

1½ tablespoons cream cheese
½ teaspoon snipped chives
1 bagel, halved
50 g (2 oz) smoked salmon
a few slices cucumber
    (optional)
a squeeze of lemon juice
freshly ground black pepper
    (optional)

Ham and cheese bagel

Butter the bagel and arrange the lettuce, cheese, ham and cucumber on top. Add a blob of mayonnaise.

🖌 3 MINUTES

🍽 1 PORTION

a little butter, softened
1 bagel, halved
a little lettuce, washed
1 large, thin slice Swiss
    cheese
1 slice ham or turkey
4 thin slices cucumber,
    washed
1 tablespoon mayonnaise

Mini bagels

2 MINUTES

2 MINI BAGELS

2 mini bagels, halved
a little softened butter
2 tablespoons light
   mayonnaise
a little iceberg lettuce,
   washed and shredded
1 tomato, washed and sliced
4 slices pastrami

Slice the bagels in half and butter them. Take two of the bagel halves and spread them with mayonnaise. Divide the lettuce between them, followed by the tomato and pastrami. Top with the remaining bagel halves.

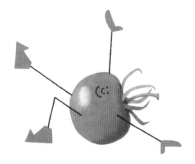

Savouries

Spanish omelette with new potato, courgette and tomato

Bring a lightly salted saucepan of water to the boil and cook the new potatoes for about 12 minutes until tender. Drain, leave to cool, then slice.

Heat the oil in a non-stick frying pan with a diameter of 18–20 cm (7–8 in). Add the onion and sauté for 2 minutes. Then add the courgette and sauté for another 6 minutes (4 minutes if using grated courgette). Add the tomatoes and cook for 2 minutes, then stir in the sliced potatoes.

Beat the eggs together with the milk, Parmesan cheese and a little seasoning. Pour the mixture over the vegetables and cook over a medium heat for about 4 minutes or until the underside of the eggs has set.

Meanwhile, preheat the grill to High. Place the frying pan under the grill (if necessary, wrap the handle with foil to prevent any damage) and cook for about 3 minutes until golden and set.

When the omelette is cold, cut into wedges and wrap in foil.

 8 MINUTES

 35 MINUTES

 6 PORTIONS

 NOT SUITABLE FOR FREEZING

100 g (3½ oz) new potatoes, washed
1 tablespoon olive oil
1 small onion, peeled and finely chopped
1 courgette, washed and chopped or grated
2 tomatoes, skinned, deseeded and roughly chopped
4 eggs
1 tablespoon milk
2 tablespoons freshly grated Parmesan cheese
salt and pepper

Tuna melt

✎ 3 MINUTES

▦ 5 MINUTES

🍴 2 PORTIONS

❄ NOT SUITABLE FOR FREEZING

200 g (7 oz) tinned tuna in
   spring water, drained
2 tablespoons tomato
   ketchup
2 tablespoons crème fraîche
1–2 spring onions, washed
   and finely sliced
2 English muffins, halved
40 g (1½ oz) Cheddar cheese,
   grated

Flake the tuna and mix together with the tomato
ketchup, crème fraîche and spring onion. Toast
the muffins, then spread with the tuna mixture
and sprinkle with the grated Cheddar cheese.
Place the muffins under a preheated grill until
the cheese is bubbling and golden.

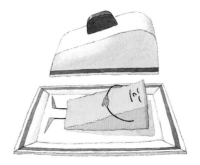

Cheese and ham muffins

Preheat the oven to 200°C/400°F/Gas 6. Line a muffin tin with 12 muffin cases.

Sieve the flour, baking powder, mustard powder and salt into a mixing bowl. Add the Cheddar cheese, ham and chives. Mix together the eggs, melted butter and milk, then add to the dry ingredients and mix until combined. Spoon the mixture into the muffin cases and sprinkle the Parmesan cheese on top.

Bake for 20–25 minutes until well risen and lightly golden.

/ 10 MINUTES
▦ 20–25 MINUTES
🍽 12 MUFFINS
❄ SUITABLE FOR FREEZING

250 g (9 oz) self-raising flour
1 teaspoon baking powder
¼ teaspoon mustard
   powder
a pinch of salt
100 g (3½ oz) mature
   Cheddar cheese, grated
100 g (3½ oz) ham, chopped
3 tablespoons chopped
   chives
2 large eggs, beaten
100 g (3½ oz) butter, melted
225 ml (7½ fl oz) milk
50 g (2 oz) Parmesan cheese,
   grated

Salad kebabs

These can be savoury or sweet. For the sticks, you can use bamboo skewers or thin plastic straws. Here are some suggestions of food combinations to thread onto the skewers.

- *Slices of ham or turkey rolled up and interspersed with cubes of cheese and wedges of pineapple*

- *Cherry tomatoes and mozzarella cheese*

- *Cucumber, carrot, red pepper and cubes of Gruyère or Emmenthal cheese*

- *Chicken tikka pieces with cucumber*

Pineapples are packed with bromelain, which can aid digestion, particularly of protein-rich foods, and help to soothe sore throats and speed up the healing of injuries.

Honey and soy chicken skewers

3 MINUTES, PLUS 1 HOUR FOR MARINATING

15 MINUTES

6 SKEWERS

NOT SUITABLE FOR FREEZING

2 tablespoons soy sauce
1 tablespoon honey
2 teaspoons orange juice
½ teaspoon dried oregano
1 tablespoon olive oil
2 chicken breast fillets, cut into strips

Put the soy sauce, honey, orange juice, oregano and olive oil into a bowl, and combine. Add the chicken and allow to marinate for 1 hour.

Preheat the oven to 220°C/430°F/Gas 7. Thread the chicken onto 6 wooden skewers. Place them on a baking sheet and roast for 15 minutes until cooked through and lightly golden.

Oriental chicken drumsticks

Put all the ingredients into a bowl. Toss together, then transfer to the fridge and leave to marinate for at least an hour, or overnight if possible.

Preheat the oven to 220°C/430°F/Gas 7. Line a baking sheet with non-stick baking paper. Tip the chicken and the marinade onto the baking sheet and bake for 30–40 minutes until cooked through and golden brown.

✏ 5 MINUTES, PLUS 1 HOUR FOR MARINATING

☐ 20 MINUTES

🍽 6 PORTIONS

❄ SUITABLE FOR FREEZING

50 ml (2 fl oz) tomato ketchup
50 ml (2 fl oz) oyster sauce
2 tablespoons soy sauce
2 tablespoons honey
1 tablespoon sunflower oil
2 garlic cloves, crushed
6–8 chicken drumsticks

Cream of tomato soup

/ 8 MINUTES

▦ 45–50 MINUTES

🍴 8 PORTIONS

❄ SUITABLE FOR FREEZING

2 tablespoons light olive oil
1 onion, peeled and chopped
1 garlic clove, crushed
2 medium carrots (200 g/
    7 oz), peeled and diced
500 g (1 lb 2 oz) ripe plum
    tomatoes, skinned,
    deseeded and roughly
    chopped
200 ml (7 fl oz) passata
    (sieved tomatoes)
400 ml (14 fl oz) vegetable
    or chicken stock
1 bay leaf
a large sprig of fresh thyme
100 ml (3½ fl oz) single
    cream (optional)
salt and pepper
a small handful of basil
    leaves (optional)

Heat the oil in a large saucepan and sauté the onion, garlic and carrots for 6–7 minutes. Stir in the tomatoes, passata, stock, bay leaf and thyme, bring to the boil, cover and simmer for 35–40 minutes. Remove the bay leaf and the thyme stalk.

Blend the soup in a food processor until smooth, stir in the cream (if using) and season with salt and pepper. You could garnish with a few basil leaves if you wish.

If you don't want to use fresh tomatoes, you can use 750 ml (1¼ pints) passata instead.

Mummy's minestrone soup

Heat the olive oil in a very large saucepan. Add the carrot, celery, onion and garlic and sauté for 10 minutes, stirring occasionally. Add the tomatoes, tomato purée and stock, bring to the boil, cover and simmer for 15 minutes.

Stir in the cabbage, basil, pasta and beans, and simmer for another 15–18 minutes until the cabbage and pasta are tender. Add seasoning, then sprinkle on the Parmesan cheese if serving at home.

Haricot beans are rich in protein, vitamins and minerals, but if your child prefers you can replace them with a tin of baked beans.

You can freeze the soup in individual containers, then defrost it overnight, heat up the soup in the morning and pour it into a flask to keep it hot until lunchtime.

12 MINUTES
45 MINUTES
8 PORTIONS
SUITABLE FOR FREEZING

2 tablespoons olive oil
1 carrot, peeled and finely diced
1 stick celery, washed and finely diced
1 small red onion, peeled and finely diced
1 garlic clove, crushed
5 ripe plum tomatoes, skinned, deseeded and roughly chopped (or 400 g/14 oz tinned chopped tomatoes)
1 tablespoon tomato purée
2 litres (4 pints) vegetable or chicken stock
100 g (3½ oz) green cabbage, washed and finely sliced
8 fresh basil leaves, torn
50 g (2 oz) small pasta shapes
400 g (14 oz) tinned haricot beans
salt and pepper
grated Parmesan cheese, grated, to serve (optional)

Chicken and corn chowder

⟋ 10 MINUTES

▦ 20 MINUTES

◔ 4 PORTIONS

✳ SUITABLE FOR FREEZING

15 g (½ oz) butter
1 large shallot (55 g/2 oz),
    peeled and finely chopped
1 medium potato, peeled
    and chopped into 1 cm
    (⅓ in) cubes
400 g (14 oz) tinned
    sweetcorn, drained
650 ml (23 fl oz) good
    chicken stock
6 tablespoons double cream
salt and pepper
50 g (2 oz) cooked chicken,
    shredded
1 tablespoon chopped
    parsley, to serve (optional)

Melt the butter in a large saucepan and sauté the shallot for 5 minutes until soft. Add the potato, sweetcorn and stock, bring to the boil and simmer until the potato is soft. Transfer half of the mixture to another container and blend, using a hand blender, until smooth. Return to the pan and stir in the double cream. Season to taste.

Stir in the chicken and sprinkle over a little parsley (if using).

For a vegetarian version, leave out the shredded chicken and use vegetable stock.

Sweet treats

Carrot and pineapple muffins

✏ 15 MINUTES

🍴 25 MINUTES

🍪 12 MUFFINS

❄ NOT SUITABLE FOR FREEZING

Preheat the oven to 180°C/350°F/Gas 4. Line a muffin tray with 12 paper cases.

Sift the flours, baking powder, bicarbonate of soda, cinnamon and salt into a large bowl and mix well. In a separate bowl, beat together the oil, sugar and eggs. Add the carrot, pineapple, raisins and pecan nuts (if using). Gradually add the flour mixture, beating until the ingredients are just combined.

Spoon the mixture into the paper cases and bake for 25 minutes. Allow the muffins to cool for a few minutes, then transfer to a wire rack.

To make the icing, beat the cream cheese together with the icing sugar. Scrape out the tiny black seeds from the vanilla pod, then stir them into the icing and spread over the tops of the muffins.

These muffins are delicious with or without the cream-cheese icing.

100 g (3½ oz) plain flour
100 g (3½ oz) plain wholemeal flour
1 teaspoon baking powder
½ teaspoon bicarbonate of soda
1½ teaspoons ground cinnamon
½ teaspoon salt
200 ml (7 fl oz) vegetable oil
100 g (3½ oz) caster sugar
2 eggs
125 g (4½ oz) carrot, peeled and finely grated
225 g (8 oz) tinned crushed pineapple, semi-drained
100 g (3½ oz) raisins
40 g (1½ oz) pecan nuts, chopped (optional)

Cream-cheese icing
175 g (6 oz) cream cheese
75 g (3 oz) icing sugar, sifted
½ vanilla pod

Apple and carrot muffins with maple syrup

 15 MINUTES

⊞ 20–25 MINUTES

🍪 12 MUFFINS

❄ SUITABLE FOR FREEZING

125 g (4½ oz) wholemeal flour

50 g (2 oz) granulated sugar

25 g (1 oz) dried skimmed-milk powder

1½ teaspoons baking powder

½ teaspoon ground cinnamon

½ teaspoon ground ginger

½ teaspoon salt

125 ml (4 fl oz) vegetable oil

3 tablespoons maple syrup

1 tablespoon honey

2 eggs, lightly beaten

½ teaspoon vanilla essence

1 large apple, peeled, cored and grated

75 g (3 oz) carrots, peeled and grated

60 g (2 oz) raisins

Preheat the oven to 180°C/350°F/Gas 4. Line a muffin tray with 12 muffin cases.

Combine the dry ingredients in a mixing bowl. In a separate bowl, mix the oil, maple syrup, honey, eggs and vanilla essence. Beat lightly with a wire whisk until blended. Add the apple, carrots and raisins and stir well. Fold in the dry ingredients until just combined, but don't overmix or the muffins will become heavy.

Spoon the mixture into the paper cases until two thirds full. Bake for 20–25 minutes. Allow to cool for a few minutes, then remove from the tray and cool on a wire rack.

Jamaican banana muffins

🖊 15 MINUTES

🍴 25–30 MINUTES

🍪 8 MUFFINS

❄ NOT SUITABLE FOR FREEZING

75 ml (2½ fl oz) sunflower oil
100 g (3½ oz) light
  muscovado sugar
250 g (9 oz) very ripe bananas
  (unpeeled weight), mashed
1 medium egg, beaten
140 g (5 oz) self-raising flour
20 g (¾ oz) wholemeal flour
½ teaspoon salt
½ teaspoon bicarbonate of
  soda
½ tablespoon ground
  cinnamon
3 tablespoons very hot water
75 g (3 oz) raisins

Topping
1 teaspoon ground cinnamon
60 g (2 oz) granulated sugar
10 g (¼ oz) butter, melted

Preheat the oven to 180°C/350°F/Gas 4. Line a muffin tin with 8 paper cases.

In a large mixing bowl, combine the sunflower oil and sugar. Add the mashed bananas and mix thoroughly. Add the egg and mix well. Sift the flours, salt, bicarbonate of soda and ground cinnamon into a medium-size bowl. Tip in the little bits that were sieved out of the wholemeal flour. Add half the flour mixture to the banana mixture and combine well. Add the hot water and mix in thoroughly. Stir in the remaining flour mixture and the raisins.

Spoon the mixture into the paper cases. Combine the topping ingredients in a small bowl and sprinkle evenly over the muffins. Bake for 25–30 minutes, or until the muffins are well risen and spring back gently when you press the tops. Transfer to a wire rack to cool.

For a gluten-free version, use 60 g (2 oz) sunflower oil, 160 g (5½ oz) gluten-free flour, 1 teaspoon bicarbonate of soda and 2 tablespoons hot milk instead of water. Bake for 30–35 minutes.

Oat and raisin cookies

Preheat the oven to 180°C/350°F/Gas 4. Line two baking sheets with non-stick paper.

Whisk the butter and sugar together until light and fluffy. Add the egg, then the remaining ingredients. Mix until well combined.

Spoon walnut-size balls onto the prepared baking sheets and put in the oven for about 14 minutes until lightly golden. Leave to cool, then remove from the baking sheets.

✎ 10 MINUTES
▦ 14 MINUTES
🍪 14 COOKIES
❄ SUITABLE FOR FREEZING

75 g (3 oz) butter, softened
75 g (3 oz) caster sugar
1 small egg, beaten
60 g (2 oz) plain flour
75 g (3 oz) raisins
35 g (1¼ oz) plain chocolate chips
50 g (2 oz) sunflower seeds
½ teaspoon bicarbonate of soda
1 teaspoon vanilla extract
a pinch of salt
40 g (1½ oz) porridge oats

Annabel's apricot cookies

🔪 10 MINUTES

🖾 15 MINUTES

🍪 18 COOKIES

❄ SUITABLE FOR FREEZING

100 g (3½ oz) unsalted butter
75 g (3 oz) cream cheese
100 g (3½ oz) caster sugar
100 g (3½ oz) plain flour
50 g (2 oz) dried apricots, chopped
65 g (2½ oz) white chocolate, chopped, or white chocolate chips

Preheat the oven to 180°C/350°F/Gas 4.

In a large mixing bowl, cream together the butter and cream cheese. Add the sugar and beat until fluffy. Gradually add the flour, then fold in the apricots and chocolate. The dough will be quite soft – don't worry! Drop heaped teaspoons of mixture onto non-stick baking sheets, or baking sheets lined with baking paper, leaving plenty of space in between them. Put the cookies in the oven for about 15 minutes, or until they are just golden.

Allow the cookies to cool and harden for a few minutes before removing them from the baking sheets.

Power-packed oat bars with cranberries, apricots and pumpkin seeds

Line and grease a 20 cm (8 in) square baking tin. Preheat the oven to 180°C/350°F/Gas 4.

In a saucepan, melt together the butter, sugar, golden syrup and salt. Mix all the dry ingredients together in a bowl and stir in the butter and syrup mixture. Spoon the mixture into the tin and press down with a potato masher to level the surface. Bake for 18–20 minutes.

Cut into bars before serving and store in the fridge.

✏ 10 MINUTES

🗓 20–25 MINUTES

🍪 12 BARS

❋ NOT SUITABLE FOR FREEZING

80 g (3 oz) butter
80 g (3 oz) brown sugar
60 g (2 oz) golden syrup
½ teaspoon salt
130 g (4½ oz) porridge oats
35 g (1¼ oz) dried apple, chopped
35 g (1¼ oz) dried apricots, chopped
25 g (1 oz) dried cranberries
25 g (1 oz) pumpkin seeds
2 tablespoons sunflower seeds
25 g (1 oz) desiccated coconut

Apple, sultana and pecan flapjacks

🔪 5 MINUTES

🗓 25–30 MINUTES

🍳 8 PORTIONS

❄ NOT SUITABLE FOR FREEZING

175 g (6 oz) butter
175 g (6 oz) brown sugar
50 g (2 oz) golden syrup
200 g (7 oz) porridge oats
50 g (2 oz) semi-dried apple,
    chopped
50 g (2 oz) sultanas
30 g (1 oz) pecan nuts,
    chopped

Preheat the oven to 160°C/320°F/Gas 3. Grease and line the base of a 20 cm (8 in) square baking tin.

Melt the butter in a saucepan. Add the sugar and syrup, and stir until dissolved. Mix in the porridge oats, fruit and nuts, and spoon into the tin. Level the top.

Bake for 20–23 minutes until just golden around the edges. Leave to cool for 5 minutes, then cut into squares or bars.

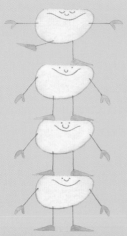

Quick and easy fruit salad

To make the orange and lemon sauce, mix the juices and stir in the sugar until dissolved.

Cut the fruit into bite-size chunks and mix with the sauce. The sauce adds flavour and stops the fruit from discolouring.

✎ 5 MINUTES

🍴 1 PORTION

❄ NOT SUITABLE FOR FREEZING

cantaloupe and honeydew melon balls
1 kiwi fruit, peeled and cut into chunks
½ mango, cut into chunks
1 thick slice of pineapple, cut into chunks
1 clementine, divided into segments

Orange and lemon sauce
2 tablespoons freshly squeezed orange juice
1 tablespoon lemon juice
2 teaspoons caster sugar

You can make delicious fruit salads using any fruits that are in season. Peel and pit the fruit if necessary. I leave the skin on fruits like apples, plums and peaches, as most of the vitamins lie just under the skin.

Great ways with fruit

Fruit on a stick
Thread a selection of fruits onto a skewer (or
thin straw for younger children). You can use
a mixture of fresh and dried fruits: for example,
kiwi fruit, pineapple, grapes, strawberries and
dried apricots.

Fruit wedges
Children like to hold wedges of fruit. Try cutting a
variety of fruits into wedges and packing them in
a plastic container with a lid. For added interest,
give a combination of fruits; pineapple, papaya
and mango go particularly well together. Fruits
that make good wedges are:

* *Mango* • *Pineapple* • *Melon* • *Orange* • *Peach*
* *Papaya* • *Pear* • *Kiwi fruit*

Left: Fruit on a stick

Index

Page numbers in **bold** indicate a recipe where entry is main ingredient

apples **82**, **90**, 91
apricots **86–9**, **93**
avocado **20**, **52**, **58**

bacon **41**
bagels **63–4**
baked beans **77**
bananas **84**
bread: types 39
broccoli **14–17**, 23, 34
bromelain 71
bulgur wheat **28**

cabbage **77**
calcium 6
carrots **25–6**, **29–31**, 52, 56, 71, **74–7**, **81–2**
celery **77**
cereal bars 9
cheese 13, **17–18**, 21, **43–4**, **52–3**, 56, 63, **67–71**, 81, 86
chicken **17–26**, **47–52**, 59, **71–3**, 78
chives 36, 63, 69
chocolate **85–6**
clementines 91
cookies **85–6**
courgettes 67
couscous **31**
cranberries 28, **89**
croutons 18
cucumber 13, 25, 29, **32–5**, 48, 56, 63, 71

digestion 71
dressings **13–27**, **29–31**, **34–5**
drinks 10

eggs **35**, **40**, **43**, **60**, **67**, 69
essential fatty acids 23

fats 6
fibre 25
flapjacks **90**
fruit 6, 9, **91–3**

grapes **93**
green beans 21, 35

ham 26, 63, **69–71**
haricot beans **77**
healthy foods 7–10
houmous **56**

immune system 23

kiwi fruit **91–3**

lettuce **18–20**, 35, **41–3**, **47–52**, 55, 64
lunchbox:
   keeping cool 11
   packing 10–11
   requirements 6–7

mangetout 23
mango **91–3**
melon **91–3**
minerals 6, 31, 77
muffins **68**, **81–4**
mustard and cress 13

noodles **25**

omega-3 fatty acids 35
onions **13–14**, 20, **24–8**, **31–4**, 36, 48, **56–60**, **67–8**, **74–7**
oranges **93**

papaya **93**
passata **74**
pasta **14–17**, 21, 26, 36, **77**
pastrami **41**, **53**, **64**
peaches 91, **93**

pears **93**
peas **17**, **32**
pecan nuts **81**, **90**
peppers **31–2**, **71**
pesto **53**
pine nuts **31**
pineapple **71**, **81**, **91–3**
plums 91
porridge oats **85**, **89–90**
potatoes **67**
prawns **40**, **58**
preparation 10–11
protein 6, 35, 77
pumpkin seeds **23**, **89**

raisins 31, **81–5**
rice **24**, **32**

salads 8, **13–36**
salmon **32–4**, 56, 63
sandwiches 7, **39–64**
   fillings 39
savouries **67–78**
shallots **78**
snacks 9
soups 8, **74–8**
starch 24
strawberries **93**
sugar snap peas 23
sultanas **90**
sunflower seeds **74**, **89**
sweet treats **81–93**
sweetcorn **14–17**, 21, **24–8**, 36, **60**, 78

tomatoes **13–14**, 20, 24, **26–8**, 35, **41–7**, 51, **53–9**, 64, 67, 71, **74–7**
   skinning 14
tortillas **47–52**
tuna **35–6**, 56, **60**, **68**
turkey **13–14**, 43, **48**, 71

vegetables 6, 7–8
vitamins 6, 25, 31, 35, 77, 91

About Annabel Karmel

Mother of three, Annabel Karmel MBE is the UK's number one parenting author and expert on devising delicious, nutritious meals for babies, toddlers and children.

Since launching with *The Complete Baby and Toddler Meal Planner* more than two decades ago, Annabel has written 37 books, which have sold over 4 million copies worldwide, covering every stage of a child's development.

With the sole aim of helping parents give their children the very best start in life, Annabel's tried-and-tested recipes have also grown into a successful supermarket food range. From delicious Organic Baby Purées to her best-selling healthy chilled meals, these offer the goodness of a home-cooked meal for those busy days.

Annabel was awarded an MBE in 2006, in the Queen's Birthday Honours, for her outstanding work in child nutrition. She also has menus in some of the largest leisure resorts in Britain and a successful app, *Annabel's Essential Guide to Feeding Your Baby and Toddler*.

For more information and recipes, visit **www.annabelkarmel.com**.

Acknowledgements

Louise Ward and Phil Carroll (Sainsbury's Books), Fiona MacIntyre, Martin Higgins and Cat Dowlett (Ebury), Dave King (photography), Tamsin Weston (props), Kate Bliman and Maud Eden (food stylists), Lucinda McCord (recipe testing), Nick Eddison and Katie Golsby (Eddison Sadd), and Sarah Smith (PR).

annabel karmel

Other titles in the series are:

ANNABEL KARMEL'S FAVOURITES

First foods

Recipes and advice to help you wean your baby

dk

Suitable from four months

ANNABEL KARMEL'S FAVOURITES

Exploring new tastes

Introduce your baby to new flavour and textures

dk

Suitable from six to nine months

ANNABEL KARMEL'S FAVOURITES

Growing independence

Healthy home-made recipes to encourage self-feeding

dk

Suitable from nine to twelve months

ANNABEL KARMEL'S FAVOURITES

Toddler meals

Nutritious recipes for your child to enjoy with the family

dk

Suitable from one year

ANNABEL KARMEL'S FAVOURITES

Tasty food for fussy kids

Great recipes to tempt your picky eater

dk

50 healthy recipes

ANNABEL KARMEL'S FAVOURITES

Family meals

Quick and easy recipes to keep meal times fresh

dk

50 healthy recipes

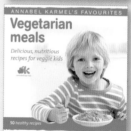

ANNABEL KARMEL'S FAVOURITES

Vegetarian meals

Delicious, nutritious recipes for veggie kids

dk

50 healthy recipes

ANNABEL KARMEL'S FAVOURITES

Party food

Quick, quirky and fun ideas for your child's celebration

dk

50 healthy recipes

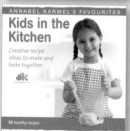

ANNABEL KARMEL'S FAVOURITES

Kids in the Kitchen

Creative recipe ideas to make and bake together

dk

50 healthy recipes